LISTENING TO MY BODY
ACTIVITIES FOR KIDS

LISTENING TO MY BODY
Activities for Kids

Social-Emotional Skills to Build
Self-Awareness and Express Feelings

BY MALLORY STRIESFELD, MS, LPC
ILLUSTRATED BY TANYA EMELYANOVA

ROCKRIDGE
PRESS

Interior and Cover Designer: Heather Krakora
Art Producer: Maya Melenchuk
Editor: Maxine Marshall
Production Editor: Nora Milman
Production Manager: Holly Haydash

Illustration © 2022 Tanya Emelyanova
Author photo courtesy of Barbara Liphor, Blip Creative Studio

Paperback ISBN: 978-1-63878-126-4
eBook ISBN: 978-1-63878-757-0
R0

This book is dedicated to:
The playrooms where children and I can explore,
To the people who dream big with me—
let's make our dreams soar.
To the challenges that helped me grow—
like you might experience, too!
This book is for anyone with big
feelings who may not know what to do.

CONTENTS

INTRODUCTION

WELCOME! I'm so glad you chose this book. Whether you're wondering what social-emotional skills are, or you're seeking resources to begin teaching these skills to young children, you are in the right place. As adults, we have had a lifetime to learn how to regulate our emotions. It can be easy to forget that children are still building these skills and need our help to do so. The good news is that you are probably already helping your child build these vital skills through the process of co-regulation.

What is co-regulation? I'm glad you asked! You know those warm, responsive interactions that you model for little ones? The interactions that help children understand and communicate their own thoughts and feelings? This is what co-regulation means—it is the ongoing process of supporting and modeling behaviors in and for the little ones around you.

You might be wondering what makes me an expert on this topic. I don't have children of my own, though I'm going through an IVF journey right now. I have hands-on caregiving experience from being an aunt since I was 12 years old, a nanny through high school and college, and a licensed mental health professional for over eight years. I have worked in preschool, nonprofit, and private settings with children, and each of these settings taught me a lot about self-regulation and co-regulation strategies.

Teaching and modeling healthy behaviors might feel like a lot of pressure, and nobody's perfect. You know what it feels like when little Sam has a meltdown in the middle of the grocery store. Rather than remaining calm, your own emotions might get the better of you. We have all been there before. Parents are humans, too, and co-regulation is not pure magic. But this book is here to help.

The activities in this book offer developmentally appropriate ways for you to build a healthy foundation of self-awareness for your little one. The information and playful activities will help you support your child as they learn to understand and manage their emotions, self-regulate, and make responsible decisions. I hope you enjoy!

1
HOW TO LISTEN TO YOUR BODY

Toddlers and preschoolers are adventurous and infinitely curious. It can be exciting and challenging for parents to watch children dive into eye-opening new experiences. During this time of discovery, children are forming the important connection between mind and body. As kids learn how body sensations and emotions connect, they need grown-ups to help them learn how to listen closely to their bodies. As adults, we can practice patience as we guide little ones through the process of connecting their minds and bodies. This chapter will prepare you for success by deepening your understanding of co-regulation and the mind-body relationship. Also, check out the handy age-by-age guide to social and emotional developmental stages for three- to five-year-olds.

Better Together: Co-Regulation for You and Your Little One

The most common question I hear from adults is: *How are you so patient with children?* My answer: co-regulation. Over the years, I have realized the power of co-regulation as a tool to keep both myself and the children I'm working with calm. For example, I've noticed that if I'm breathing slowly and calmly (as with the "dragon breathing" skill, which we will cover in a chapter 2 activity), the child next to me will be breathing calmly, too. When I'm aware of my body and how emotions affect each part of it, not only can I manage my own concerns that might bring me stress—like dealing with type 1 diabetes, for example—but I can also model this for the child next to me.

Kids can't do this on their own yet—they still need adults to support them in building these life skills. This is why children have meltdowns when they don't get their way. They're unable to regulate their emotions or channel them into productive outlets when life doesn't go as planned. How can grown-ups help with this? Take a moment, breathe, and remain present and calm with your child. This is one way for you to practice self-regulation, which can lead to successful co-regulation for you and your little one!

I know this isn't a foolproof plan. It won't always work in the moment. The overall goal is to support your kiddo's social and emotional development in such a way that they're able to do this naturally over time. Not many things are overnight miracles, and development takes time. Together, we can pave the way for our little ones to practice healthy engagement and develop their own self-regulation skills.

Self-Regulation through Co-Regulation

We can support our children in so many ways by teaching them how to self-regulate. When Katherine looks across the room at her daughter, Gigi, she instantly smiles and laughs. Gigi begins smiling and laughing back. This is an example of reflecting. Look at some of the ways we can support kids using co-regulation strategies!

Label. Help kids express their emotions by pairing feeling words (like excitement or sadness) with body sensations (like an upset tummy or tight throat).

Model. Consciously display behaviors that you'd like your child to emulate, like waiting patiently or being respectful.

Reflect. Show emotions on your face when you notice what others are feeling, like smiling big when your child happily hugs your legs—you can be a mirror to help your child see and reflect on their own emotions.

Redirect. Offer choices to help little ones take a different path or redirect strong emotions. (Stick to only two or three choices, or little brains might get overwhelmed!)

Be consistent. Provide predictability in little ones' lives to help them feel confident when taking on challenges and tough emotions.

Make plans. Show kids—with pictures or sounds—what is coming next in their routine.

Validate. Help little ones name what you see and hear them experiencing—teach them words to name their big feelings.

Support. Build safe and fun environments where little ones feel welcome and safe.

Do kids pick up on what we do? Four-year-old Xavier waits with Nana at her doctor's appointment. Xavier declares, "I'm bored!" Nana decides to redirect Xavier's attention by showing him the books and toys in the corner of the office while they wait. Nana and Xavier begin reading a book together. When the nurse calls Nana into the doctor's office, Nana calmly explains the plan for Xavier to follow her and the nurse. Xavier listens and hears Nana ask the nurse a few questions.

Xavier sees how Nana remains calm when the nurse pricks her arm for blood. When the doctor enters, Xavier begins feeling nervous because the last time he was in the doctor's office, he had to get shots! Xavier feels his heart beating faster and his tummy filling up with butterflies. Rather than crying, he begins taking a deep breath like he's seen Nana do. He nervously asks the doctor, "Am I going to get a shot today?" The doctor smiles and laughs while shaking his head "no." When Xavier sees Nana and the doctor smiling, he smiles, too. Xavier is not only demonstrating self-regulation, but he is also highlighting that co-regulation occurs when he trusts his Nana, a positive role model in his life.

Understanding Sensations and Feelings

Feelings are created by our thoughts and emotions, while sensations are what we physically feel in our bodies. For example, you and your child are on the beach feeling wind in your hair. That is a physical sensation. Sensations engage all five of our senses: sight, touch, taste, smell, and sound. When we're on the beach, we experience the sensations of seeing the ocean, smelling the salty air, touching the sand, and hearing crashing waves. We might taste the PB & J we brought for lunch, or a bit of salt water.

Now, let's say you're watching a scary movie. You start feeling butterflies in your stomach, maybe you're sweating, and your hands are clammy. These are physical sensations your body displays in response to emotion—in this case, anxiety or fear. Feelings have a cause-and-effect reaction to them that can be challenging for children to understand within their bodies. Learning where these sensations come from, along with the feelings they pair within each child's body, is vital for their early developmental success.

How can we help? Let's start off with 50 different sensation and feeling words you can use with your little ones at home. This is a great place to start building their vocabulary so they can understand, name, and express what they are feeling. As your child learns and grows, you can expand this list to include new words.

SENSATIONS:

- Achy
- Breathless
- Burning
- Clammy
- Cold
- Dizzy
- Energized
- Fluttery
- Full
- Hungry
- Itchy
- Shaky
- Shivery
- Smiling
- Sore
- Sweaty
- Tense
- Thirsty
- Tingly
- Tired
- Trembly
- Twitchy
- Warm
- Weak
- Wobbly

FEELINGS:

- Angry
- Annoyed
- Bored
- Brave
- Calm
- Caring
- Cautious
- Confident
- Confused
- Disappointed
- Energetic
- Friendly
- Grumpy
- Guilty
- Interested
- Jealous
- Joyful
- Lonely
- Overwhelmed
- Proud
- Scared
- Silly
- Surprised
- Thoughtful
- Worried

Don't worry if this list feels overwhelming now, or if some of the words don't feel applicable for your child yet. Every child is different. Will your child have the same vocabulary as their friend? Probably not! Each child learns at a different pace. We are simply here to support them and act as healthy models who our children can learn from each day.

Here's the main goal: We want our little ones to begin learning how to differentiate between physical sensations and their feelings. As we move forward into the activities shared in the following chapters, this skill will help your child! Many of the activities are focused on supporting little ones as they learn to decipher sensations and feelings. This vocabulary list is merely an introduction to help you get started and best use these activities to support your child's growth.

The Sensation-Feeling Connection

Let's get into the nitty-gritty of how our body sensations and feelings connect. When we want to increase our emotional intelligence, it often comes down to increasing our self-awareness about the physical sensations behind our emotions.

When we're able to step back and pay attention to what our bodies are trying to communicate, we can have a better understanding of why we feel the way we feel. What activates sensations? Our feelings stimulate the sensations we feel within our bodies, especially when we have strong emotions! Learning this important connection impacts the way we respond to situations and the choices we make.

Our brains are wired to react. For example, imagine you are driving down the road and the person in the lane beside you cuts you off. This startles you and makes you very angry; you are tired and at the end of a long day. Your brain's first response—without thinking—might be to engage in unhealthy behaviors, including making rude gestures, honking your horn, yelling, or driving aggressively.

Now let's say that, instead of acting without pausing to think, you listen to your body first. You notice you're feeling flushed, you're gripping the steering wheel harder than before, and your shoulders are close to your ears, locked and tight. Your body is sending a signal to your brain, activating the emotion associated with those physical reactions. You realize that you are angry or upset. Now you have given yourself time to make choices about how to respond to the situation. Our brain has the power to do all of that quickly, if we practice.

When children begin to understand how their bodies connect with their emotions, they learn the important skills such as how to self-regulate, problem-solve creatively, and make healthy choices. These abilities also translate into helping others, having empathy, and developing positive self-esteem. So, what are we waiting for? Let's start making these sensation-feeling connections!

Every Child Is Beautifully Different

These days, I meet a lot of children who love unicorns and narwhals. I believe kids love these magical-seeming animals because they embrace the differences they see in others. Imaginary creatures like unicorns capture the beauty of difference. This is a beauty we should celebrate. Every child develops in different ways and at their own pace. No matter where your child is in their journey, don't worry; the activities here are designed to be adaptable to meet your child's needs in this moment. Take note of your child's strengths and needs so that you can adjust the activities as needed. Some challenges and special needs that are common for kids ages three to five include:

Developmental delays. If your child takes longer to meet certain milestones, it can sometimes be more challenging to feel calm when your child gets upset. They may be quicker to anger and harder to soothe than others their age. Adapt activities to meet the needs of your child by replacing words with more visual cues. This helps children have more independence while building their emotional vocabulary.

Autism spectrum disorder. Children who are diagnosed along the spectrum can struggle with social cues and self-control. Though we engage our five senses for these activities, this might be a challenge for your little one. To avoid overwhelming your child, try pulling back on sensory stimuli that they are sensitive to. For example, if your child doesn't like a cotton ball touching their face, change the activity to use a different object or a different sense.

Cognitive or physical disabilities. Though children with cognitive or physical disabilities may require extra support for some activities, it's important for them to be able to explore the world through their senses. Talk them through the steps and give them extra time to think about or complete the activities, if needed.

Chronic illness. Kids diagnosed with chronic illness are often required to listen to their body sensations. This might mean that children with chronic illness are more skilled at noticing the signals their bodies are sending. Adapt activities to include different movements and energy levels, when needed.

An Age-by-Age Guide to Success

Children grow up so quickly! Between the ages of three and five, major things happen. Each child is full of wonder, curiosity, and independence, with their own capabilities and limitations unique to them. Let's explore these developmental ages and stages in more detail:

Three-Year-Olds

I can do it myself. This is a sentiment that your three-year-old will start to express, if they haven't already. Our little ones still crave routines, even with their newfound independence and awareness of others. At this age, kids are not afraid to ask "why?" when they're unsure. Though they may not enjoy it, kids are learning how to share with their friends while forming more permanent memories.

CAPABILITIES AND LIMITATIONS

- **Attention span.** Most experts agree that a child can pay attention for 2 to 3 minutes per year of age. For three-year-olds, this would mean that they can focus on a single activity for 6 to 9 minutes. Right now, children can focus on following instructions that include more than one step. When you have your child's eye contact, it's safe to say you have their attention.

- **Language/communication.** Three-year-olds are little chatterboxes! They are constantly asking "why?" Kids this age are learning to express their needs and wants in helpful ways, unless they're really frustrated!

- **Social/emotional.** Three-year-olds are showing empathy, beginning to play with friends, and learning how to label basic emotions, such as happy, sad, and angry. They are forming friendships, but they may need help navigating them.

Four-Year-Olds

Not only does our optic nerve fully develop at four years but so does our personality! Have you been wondering how your child became so incredibly bossy overnight? Did you get overwhelmed when they went to preschool, and suddenly your child could form complex sentences? That's right, your little one turned four!

CAPABILITIES AND LIMITATIONS

- **Attention span.** The average four-year-old has an 8- to 12-minute attention span. Though their attention is growing, kids may still have tantrums or struggle with routine changes.

- **Language/communication.** Your four-year-old is likely very talkative. This can be cute when they're singing silly songs and telling jokes. It's not as adorable when they begin telling you small lies as a form of communication and boundary testing.

- **Social/emotional.** Most four-year-olds can show a wider range of emotions, talk about what they're thinking, and create stories. Friendships are more important now, especially best friends! Children are becoming problem-solvers, as they're now able to successfully share and take turns. However, they may start illogical arguments that can be counterproductive to healthy problem-solving.

Five-Year-Olds

This is the year that many children begin attending kindergarten! Kids are continuing to grow up so fast, and right now, they're doing everything they can to please their friends and loved ones. Many five-year-olds understand right from wrong. By developing this skill, kids can often resolve conflict without needing help from grown-ups.

CAPABILITIES AND LIMITATIONS

- **Attention span.** Most five-year-olds are now able to attend to tasks for 10 to 15 minutes at a time. They can sit for longer amounts of time in classroom settings while listening to instructions.

- **Language/communication.** At this age, we can understand our children more clearly. They're also directly telling others their wants and needs. This can help little ones carry on meaningful conversations with others, even at a young age. The challenge is that sometimes their language may sound demanding.

- **Social/emotional.** Many five-year-olds begin voicing their feelings in deeper ways. For example, *"I don't like it when I have to . . ."* They also have increasing gender awareness, understand the difference between fantasy and reality, and want more privacy with friends. Kids still prefer pretend play at this stage and are more agreeable with friends' rules.

How to Use This Book

This book is divided into five types of activities designed to help littles ones pay closer attention to their bodies. These are developmentally appropriate for children ages three to five years old who like to have fun! Remember that every child is different, and you should feel free to adapt or skip activities to meet your child's needs in the moment. Let's have some fun with feelings from head to toe, shall we?

If your child chooses not to engage or becomes resistant for any reason, offer them time and space. Please don't force any of these activities on your little one. It is okay to try again another time. This will make sure that you are creating space for pleasant feelings rather than yucky ones. Children should feel empowered to say, "I decide!"

Within each of the chapters, the activities are arranged from simple to complex, with a list of materials and the preparation time you'll need. Each activity is ranked with a messiness rating from 0 (no cleanup required) to 3 (15+ minutes of cleanup needed). As a bonus, each activity includes one of these three tips:

◆ Age Adaptation: adjusts the activity for different age ranges

◆ Simple Swap: adapts the activity within a new setting/environment

◆ Get Creative: expands the activity to include different materials

Most of these activities are designed to be simple, repetitive, and fun for your little one! It's up to you to keep your child's abilities in mind when choosing how many activities to do each day. The great thing is that your child can choose what they love, taking the ones that are helpful and leaving the ones that aren't. Every child is different!

2

HEAD TO TOE

～～～～～～

ne of the best things about being a child is having fun while playing, especially when play includes movement and even learning! One of the most important things your child is working on is learning how to feel their feelings in appropriate ways. That starts by knowing how feelings such as joy, anger, and excitement feel in their bodies. The activities in this chapter will help you and your little one playfully engage together to discover how our bodies feel during little and big emotions. From the bottom of those growing feet to the top of those big brains, take a moment and truly enjoy this time together!

NAME THAT FEELING!

Children become more aware by using their minds to connect feelings with their bodies. Let's help kids have fun by pairing words with actions!

MATERIALS:

NONE

STEPS:

1. Your child can either sit or stand for this game.

2. Explain to your child that you will both be choosing feeling words and acting out big emotions with your faces!

3. Start by choosing a feeling word for your little one (like happy, sad, tired, angry).

4. For each word, ask your child to make the biggest feeling face they know how to make using that feeling. Then have them wiggle their whole body to act out the emotion!

5. Take turns, alternating between you and your child choosing the feeling for the other to act out. Have fun playing together!

AGE ADAPTATION: Level up this activity for older children by asking them to tell a story about a time they felt the feeling you're talking about.

THE BUNNY HOP DANCE

Sometimes we feel excited, and our hearts beat fast. At other times, we're resting, and our hearts are calm. By pairing fast movements with fun, familiar music, kids can begin to understand how to control their bodies. Creating a dance is a great way to practice self-control while also noticing differences in how our bodies are feeling. Who's ready to hop along?

STEPS:

1. Start by asking your little one to stand with you in an open space with room to move around.

2. Explain to your child that for the next few moments, you both get to hop and dance like bunnies!

3. Turn on the music. Each of you will create a bunny hop dance to a familiar song with a fast rhythm. If your child has a favorite song in mind they can choose that one!

4. After the dance, ask your child to lay on the floor with you and place their hand over their heart.

5. Ask your child what they're noticing within their body. Is their heart beating fast or slow? Now wait 2 minutes. Do they notice a difference in their body?

MATERIALS:

FAMILIAR SONG WITH A FAST RHYTHM, SUCH AS "HAPPY" BY PHARRELL WILLIAMS

GET CREATIVE: Invite your child to create and name their own animal character to do this dance—it can even be an imaginary creature!

POM-POM CHECK-IN

The sense of touch helps us explore the world and feel connected with each other in healthy ways. Children rely on trusted adults to help them understand these sensations. The soothing sensation of a soft object will calm your child in ways that capture their attention.

MATERIALS:

LARGE CRAFT
POM-POM

STEPS:

1. Begin by asking your little one if they'd like to sit in your lap or beside you for this activity.

2. Take a large craft pom-pom and explain to your child that you will be "checking in" with different parts of their body while rubbing the soft pom-pom against their skin.

3. Start at the top of your child's head and check in with each part of their body that is safe and appropriate. When rubbing the pom-pom over each body part, ask your little one how each part is feeling today (e.g., "How is your tummy feeling after snack time?").

4. If your child has a certain area that has a scrape or hurts more than other parts, spend more time and attention on this area of the body.

SIMPLE SWAP: Use any soft object you have, such as a cotton ball or pipe cleaner. Your child can even choose from two different objects!

MOVE LIKE AN ANIMAL

Using creativity and imagination, we can actively encourage children to use different body movements to explore their feelings. For example, a dinosaur stomp might show anger or excitement.

STEPS:

1. Find an empty square tissue box and help your child cover it with their favorite construction paper and glue—like wrapping a gift!

2. Together, you and your kiddo can draw animal pictures on each side of the box—there are six total. Decorate with sticks, colored tape, or markers for added fun.

3. With your child, write an action that each animal does underneath the picture they drew (e.g., Stomp like a dinosaur!).

4. Roll the cube and do your best animal movements and sounds!

5. Before your turn is finished, complete the sentence: "I feel like _____, when I stomp like a dinosaur."

MATERIALS:

SQUARE TISSUE BOX

CONSTRUCTION PAPER

KID-FRIENDLY SCISSORS

GLUE OR GLUE STICK

CRAYONS

OPTIONAL: TAPE, WASHABLE MARKERS, STICKERS

AGE ADAPTATION: Incorporate self-regulation games such as red light/green light into this activity to help older children practice stopping and starting their bodies.

DOUGHY HANDS

Children explore their world through touch. We will use playdough for this activity to activate different senses in our bodies.

MATERIALS:

2 CONTAINERS OF PLAYDOUGH

FLAT SURFACE

STEPS:

1. Have your child choose their favorite color of playdough for themselves and have them choose one for you! Use your hands or a flat surface like a table or tray.

2. Begin by slowly working the playdough into a familiar shape, like a ball or worm. Do this slowly and mindfully. If your child starts moving their hands quickly, model what you're doing to remind them to slow their bodies down.

3. While you're both creating your shapes, ask your little one how their body is feeling. Is their heart beating fast or slow? Are they feeling happy, frustrated, or excited?

4. Now have them create a different familiar shape quickly! How does their body feel now?

5. Repeat this activity using different speeds. Encourage your child to create words for how fast or slow you're moving!

GET CREATIVE: Add a scent to the playdough to stimulate another sense, using household items like herbs, lemon juice, chocolate powder, or vanilla flavoring.

DRAGON BREATHING

Help your child take a few fiery breaths to calm their body down naturally. All you need is your body and a few feeling words to help share your magical experiences.

STEPS:

1. For this activity, you only need your body!

2. Tell your child that you're going to practice calming your bodies by breathing like dragons.

3. You and your little one will breathe in through your noses and let out a fiery exhale with a roar through your mouths.

4. Repeat this three to five times.

5. Ask your child how their body feels now after their fiery dragon breaths!

MATERIALS:

NONE

GET CREATIVE: Get silly with it! Fold your arms like wings as you breathe. Stick your tongue out on the exhale! You can even name your dragon!

3
FUN WITH FEELINGS

~~~~~~~~~~~~~~~~~~~~~~~~~~~~~~~~~~~~~

Young children are learning what it's like to experience different feelings—sometimes more than one feeling at once. Our job is to support our little ones in learning to manage the feelings in their growing bodies. The following activities will assist you in helping your child identify and manage gigantic and tiny feelings alike, with games that encourage kids to practice patience, self-control, and self-expression.

BURST MY BUBBLES

Our bodies feel many emotions. When we're angry, we might feel like dragons breathing fire from our noses! We might feel butterflies in our bellies when we get nervous or stressed. Let's use bubbles to practice blowing away the feelings we don't want anymore.

MATERIALS:

BUBBLE SOLUTION
AND WAND

STEPS:

1. Ask your child to join you in their favorite outdoor space. Open the container of bubbles.

2. Ask your little one to close their eyes. Have them search for a feeling in their body that they would like to blow away into the air. They might feel their stomach doing nervous flip-flops or angry feet wanting to kick the ground.

3. Invite your child to open their eyes and dip the wand into the bubble container. Have them pretend they're dipping the wand into any sad or angry feelings inside their body.

4. Ask your little one to take a long, deep breath, then let it out slowly as they blow the bubbles. They will use their breath to blow angry, nervous, or sad feelings away from their body, like blowing out birthday candles.

5. Watch the bubbles float away into the air. Does your child's body feel calm?

GET CREATIVE: Create homemade bubbles with dish detergent, cornstarch, baking powder, glycerin, and distilled water.

MY LION'S DEN

In this activity, you and your child will enjoy creative play while managing your feelings like lions. Imagine you are both lions who feel happy, sad, angry, tired, sleepy, brave, or hungry.

STEPS:

1. Give your child a paper plate with kid-friendly scissors. Together, cut out the center of the plate.

2. Have your child cut long strips of red, yellow, and brown construction paper for their lion's mane.

3. Your little one can decorate their own lion mask with colored paper strips using glue or a glue stick. Glue the strips around the edge of the plate so that they will flop around your child's face like a mane.

4. Use the mask to act out different feelings a lion may feel, like being brave, calm, angry, or tired. Don't forget to let out your best roars!

GET CREATIVE: Create a den for your little lion using things around their room, like pillows, blankets, and stuffed animals.

MATERIALS:

PAPER PLATES

KID-FRIENDLY SCISSORS

RED, YELLOW, AND BROWN CONSTRUCTION PAPER

GLUE OR GLUE STICK

FIRECRACKER POPS

Sometimes we must find ways to control our bodies when we feel big emotions. This activity will help pair physical movement with feelings that can start tiny in our bodies and grow over time. Before we know it, we snap, crackle, and pop like firecrackers! Let's try managing our bodies in a fun way!

MATERIALS:

NONE

STEPS:

1. Begin by discussing with your child that feelings can start tiny and then explode like firecrackers. Some of these feelings include excitement, anger, and surprise.

2. You and your child should sit in a tight squatting position. Your arms will be giving your knees a nice warm hug.

3. On the count of three, you and your child will jump into the air as high as you can, reaching your hands and arms up high!

4. You'll land back in a squatting position with your arms giving your knees another tight hug.

5. Put it all together and repeat five times!

SIMPLE SWAP: Try doing this activity after quiet time, to tell your bodies that it's time to start moving again!

READY, SET, FREEZE!

For this activity, we're pairing our sense of hearing with self-control. Most young children have difficulty stopping their bodies when they're having fun. This game helps little ones practice controlling their dance moves. Soon, their bodies will begin to recognize how to stop more quickly.

STEPS:

1. Have your child pick a familiar song. If they can't choose, suggest a kid-friendly song that will be fun to dance to.

2. When the music begins, everyone will start dancing any way they choose. This can get silly very quickly!

3. When the music stops, everyone freezes like a statue! Wait until the music begins again, then start dancing. This continues until the song is over.

4. Anyone who moves after the song stops must complete the following sentence: "I feel _____ when I stop dancing."

MATERIALS:

FAMILIAR SONG(S)

AGE ADAPTATION: Freezing for longer periods of time will challenge older children who can already control their bodies.

FEELINGS CHARADES

Explore combining actions and feelings to engage your child in practicing different emotions. Make really big facial expressions and body movements when you play this game!

MATERIALS:

BLANK PAPER

PEN OR PENCIL

BOWL

OPTIONAL: KID-FRIENDLY SCISSORS

STEPS:

1. Tear or cut a piece of paper into six to eight pieces. Give half the pieces to your child.

2. Together, write a feeling either of you feel or have felt before on each piece of paper.

3. Fold the papers and mix them up in the bowl.

4. Choose a feeling word and act it out until the other person guesses it correctly!

5. Take turns until all the paper slips are gone.

AGE ADAPTATION: Help older children write down more complex feelings, such as disappointment and frustration.

TAKE FIVE!

With practice, this activity can help little ones build self-control. It is designed to help your child's body build impulse control by taking a short pause before talking.

STEPS:

1. Begin by tearing or cutting the sheet of paper into smaller pieces for you and your child to write questions on.

2. Take turns brainstorming questions together. Make sure some of them focus on how we feel, and then throw in some silly questions for fun!

3. Choose who will ask the first question. The other person will answer. Then take turns.

4. Here's the catch—use a timer and before anyone can answer their question, you must wait a full 5 seconds!

5. After 5 seconds, you're allowed to say the answer! If you or your child answers before the timer is finished, the other person wins that round. Then the game starts over. Don't forget to have a blast!

AGE ADAPTATION: Have four- and five-year-old kiddos wait 10 seconds longer than three-year-olds to practice self-control strategies.

MATERIALS:

BLANK PAPER

SAND TIMER OR PHONE TIMER

OPTIONAL: KID-FRIENDLY SCISSORS

4

I FEEL, YOU FEEL, WE ALL FEEL

Your child is just beginning to learn how to see an idea through someone else's perspective. Kids' brains aren't quite developed enough to focus on many people outside of themselves. Young children need extra support to help with perspective-taking and practicing empathy. The activities in this chapter are designed to engage children in creative ways to help them understand that it's okay to think and feel differently from others, so long as we are aware of how it impacts those around us.

I LIKE ME!

Believe it or not, compliments can be tough for kids to receive. As children are learning to be kind to others, we want to show how they can display kindness to themselves as well. In this activity, you'll help your child identify what they like about themselves with a social-emotional connection.

MATERIALS:

BLANK PAPER

FAVORITE WRITING UTENSIL

STEPS:

1. Begin by talking to your little one about compliments. We can offer compliments to others or even ourselves!

2. Tell your child that today you get to be kindness keepers. This means that you will model for your child how to offer compliments to themselves by saying, "I like _____ about me!"

3. Get a piece of paper and your child's favorite writing utensil to start creating an awesome compliment list. You and your child can add to this list whenever you think of a great compliment.

4. When you state a compliment about yourself or each other, talk about what it feels like to accept a compliment. Does your body want to accept what you're saying or throw it away?

GET CREATIVE: Hang the list as a poster in your little one's room. Get creative with decorations and colors.

MESSINESS:	PREP TIME:	ACTIVITY TIME:
1	5 to 7 minutes	5 minutes

KINDNESS PUPPETS

This activity helps children think about other people's feelings by imagining a puppet's perspective. Have fun taking turns role-playing scenarios to practice perspective-taking.

STEPS:

1. Think and talk about the power of words with your child.

2. Create your own sock puppets using white tube socks and markers. You can also use materials like pipe cleaners and googly eyes, if available.

3. Create a role-play scenario with your child where one puppet accidentally hurts the other puppet's feelings. The first puppet then offers kind words. Now take turns practicing this.

4. Let's check in with our bodies! What do kind words, rather than hurtful ones, feel like?

MATERIALS:

PAIR OF WHITE TUBE SOCKS

MARKERS

OPTIONAL: GLUE, PIPE CLEANERS, GOOGLY EYES, AND OTHER DECORATIVE MATERIALS

SIMPLE SWAP: Use paper bags to create your puppets! These are a great substitute if socks aren't available.

CHOOSE A SHOE

Do you or your child ever wonder what it's like to walk a day in someone else's shoes? In this activity, you both get to pretend and create your own story! Where will these shoes take you?

MATERIALS:

SEVERAL DIFFERENT PAIRS OF SHOES

STEPS:

1. Go on an adventure around the house to find pairs of shoes in all shapes and sizes.

2. Tell your child that today you're making up a story. They will choose a pair of shoes and create a main character to wear them.

3. Put the shoes on to really make the story come to life! What does it feel like to walk in someone else's shoes?

4. Choose a different pair of shoes and try it again!

GET CREATIVE: On a sunny day, take this activity outside! Children will be able to see the shadows of big and small shoes.

THE ULTIMATE MAZE CHALLENGE

Sometimes our kids have different ideas than we do. Let's turn this into a learning opportunity! In this activity, your child may choose to do things a different way than you. Let's celebrate our differences in thinking and feeling while helping each other understand.

STEPS:

1. Grab a container of toy blocks or bricks.

2. Side by side with your little one, create mazes with the blocks.

3. It's a race! Set a timer for 5 minutes. You each will create the ultimate maze.

4. Look at both of your mazes! We all have different ideas about how things can look and how to solve a problem. Tell each other about your maze ideas and how you decided what to build.

MATERIALS:

PLASTIC INTERLOCKING TOY BLOCKS (SUCH AS LEGOS, DUPLO, OR MEGA BLOKS)

SAND TIMER, STOPWATCH, OR PHONE TIMER

AGE ADAPTATION: For most three-year-olds, using foam blocks can enhance sensory awareness. Try these instead of hard construction blocks.

STORYBOOK SPIES

Sometimes when we're looking at others' perspectives, we really need to be paying close attention. In this activity, you'll help your little one identify how their favorite characters are thinking and feeling by becoming super sleuths together!

MATERIALS:

FAMILIAR BOOK

STEPS:

1. Choose a favorite or familiar storybook with your child.

2. Reading it this time will be different! Tell your child that you're going to be supersecret spies!

3. Remember, spies must be quiet so they don't get caught. Every few pages, softly ask your child how the characters might be thinking and feeling. How might your child help the character feel better?

GET CREATIVE: Find or create supersecret spy glasses to wear as you observe the characters in the book together!

MESSINESS:	PREP TIME:	ACTIVITY TIME:
0	None	5 minutes

GREETINGS, EARTHLING!

Young children are increasing their social awareness. This includes understanding how to interact with others. In this activity, your child will practice social skills by seeing things from an earthling's point of view.

STEPS:

1. Congratulations! You and your child have landed your spaceship on planet Earth! Now you get to choose how to greet the humans.

2. What does your body feel comfortable with? Discuss this with your little one and create some fun options for possible greetings from your home planet.

3. You and your child may choose to fist bump or elbow bump, use jazz hands, or create a secret handshake. When you choose your greeting, practice it with each other.

4. Take turns sharing how your body feels after offering the greeting. Think about how the earthlings feel when you greet them!

MATERIALS:

NONE

AGE ADAPTATION: We greet family members differently than we greet friends and strangers. Challenge older children to create different greetings for family, friends, and strangers.

5

PLAY WELL WITH OTHERS

H as your child ever come home with the important news that they have a new best friend? These kinds of statements help you know that it is time to support them in building relationship skills and boundaries. The activities in this chapter serve as a guide to support your little one in connecting body sensations with learning responses to social situations. Practice resolving conflict, respectfully disagreeing, trusting each other, and using problem-solving skills, all while having some fun together!

THANKFUL TIME

Showing appreciation is paired with the feeling of thankfulness. For our children to know this, we should teach and model it for them. Use this time and space to show your little one how to have an attitude of gratitude.

MATERIALS:

NONE

STEPS:

1. Sit on the floor or a comfortable space together.

2. Explain the feeling of gratitude/thankfulness we can have toward family and friends and how that feels in our heart.

3. Take turns reflecting on who or what you're thankful for and why by saying, "I'm thankful for _____ because _____."

4. Repeat this three times. Remember to help your little one stay present! It's tempting to say the same things or people every time, so you may have to challenge them.

AGE ADAPTATION: It might help young kids stay focused if you take a thankful walk during this activity to get their bodies moving.

DO YOU AGREE?

It can feel hard to disagree with someone we care about. If children don't express their opinions, they can grow up feeling unheard by others. In this activity, help your little one understand that it's okay to respectfully disagree.

STEPS:

1. Choose an outdoor space or open a window in your home with your child.

2. Listen to different familiar sounds in nature together.

3. You and your child will take turns guessing what you think the noise sounds like.

4. When you or your child have a new idea, practice saying, "I respectfully disagree. I think that sounds like a/an _____."

5. What does your body feel like when someone disagrees with you?

MATERIALS:

NONE

SIMPLE SWAP: Rather than using sounds, you can activate the sense of touch by placing everyday objects in an empty shoebox with a lid and reaching in.

SHHH . . . BALL

This activity brings together many of the skills we practiced in chapter 4, including self-control and patience. Here, your little one will practice taking turns and building self-awareness through knowing where their body is in relation to the ball.

MATERIALS:

SOFT, SAFE BALL

STEPS:

1. Stand with your child in a large open space.

2. Have your child choose a soft, safe ball to throw with you.

3. For 2 to 3 minutes, throw the ball back and forth to each other. There's one golden rule, though—no one can talk!

4. If anyone drops the ball, the other picks it up and starts the game over again until time runs out.

5. After the game, discuss with your child what it's like not being able to talk during a game. Is it frustrating or helpful? Did you want to talk a lot or a little? Did your body feel stressed or calm?

AGE ADAPTATION: For older children who can often handle more stimuli, add another ball to build frustration tolerance!

ZOMBIE WALK

It's tough to not feel in control of our own bodies! Let's explore building trusting relationships while becoming brand-new zombies with our little ones. Since we can't use some of our senses, we must depend a lot on our ears and noses during this activity.

STEPS:

1. Choose a safe, wide-open area to walk in.

2. You and your child will take turns becoming a zombie! Remember, as a brand-new zombie, you can't see yet. Yikes! Take turns closing your eyes or wearing a blindfold.

3. This means the other person will have to tell you where to go and how to move your body. You have to keep your eyes closed and trust your partner to give directions where to go and what to do.

4. Talk about what it's like to not have control and listen to someone else.

AGE ADAPTATION: Stick to single-step instructions for three-year-olds. Older kids can handle multiple steps, such as "go to the right, then take 10 steps and sit down."

MATERIALS:
OPTIONAL: BLINDFOLD

DON'T BREAK THE SNAKE!

This activity will support your child with problem-solving in helpful and creative ways. Did the first way not work? Don't worry, you can find another way to solve it when you work together—even if you get a bit frustrated sometimes.

MATERIALS:

2 CONTAINERS OF PLAYDOUGH

FLAT SURFACE

STEPS:

1. Grab two containers of playdough—one each for you and your child to use on a safe, flat surface.

2. Direct your child to use their playdough to create the longest snake they can without breaking it—and you'll do the same.

3. If either of your snakes break, it's okay! This is a chance to model problem-solving. Sometimes things break, and we can fix them. How can we fix the snake together?

4. Discuss how your child feels in the moment if the snake breaks or doesn't break.

GET CREATIVE: Have your kiddo choose what they'd like to create! Chances are they will choose something more challenging, which gives you more modeling opportunities.

FRIENDSHIP ROCKS

Kindness comes in all shapes and sizes! By helping your kiddo show acts of kindness to friends and loved ones, you are encouraging healthy social development and relationships to form.

STEPS:

1. Collect a few palm-size, smooth rocks to decorate.

2. Ask your child to think about one or two friends or loved ones. You can help them with a prompt if needed. (Example: "I've been thinking about _____ because _____. They make me feel _____.")

3. Now take out the art supplies and start decorating your rocks to give those friends! They can be decorated however you'd like. There are no rules for this one!

MATERIALS:

4 OR 5 PALM-SIZE SMOOTH ROCKS

PAINT (WATERCOLOR OR ACRYLIC)

PAINTBRUSHES

OPTIONAL: PAINT PENS

SIMPLE SWAP: Take this activity outside to your child's favorite spot and have a picnic lunch!

6

I DECIDE

~~~~~~~~~~~~~~~~~~~~

Decisions are not only a big part of growing up, but they're also a huge part of life. Each day, we make choices that can turn out to be helpful or not so healthy. Children are still learning about how their bodies feel when making important decisions, as well as how to navigate any potential consequences. This chapter supports children learning how to pay closer attention to their bodies, helping them read the cues to make healthy choices.

I CHOOSE MY STORY

Sometimes you read a story and don't agree with the character's decisions, or you don't care for the ending of a book. Chances are, this happens to your child, too. This activity turns that frustration into a learning experience. When you get to choose your own storybook ending, anything is possible.

MATERIALS:

UNFAMILIAR BOOK

STEPS:

1. Help your child pick an unfamiliar book that you haven't yet read or don't read often.

2. Together, read the first few pages aloud.

3. Stop reading and offer two different paths the main character can decide to take.

4. Have your child choose one option and create their own storybook ending based on their choice!

5. Remember, this is a chance to talk about the character's feelings as they're on the journey your child chooses for them.

GET CREATIVE: Rather than suggesting two different paths at the beginning of the story, read further, then discuss two alternate endings.

SUPERHEROES VS. MONSTERS

In this game of imagination, help your child teach the monsters who's boss! Offering them playful choices can support our little ones in making decisions and learning about consequences in healthy ways.

STEPS:

1. Oh no! Monsters are taking over your city! It's time for you and your child to become superheroes and make some choices.

2. Help guide your child in imagining two different ways to defeat the monsters with safe items you have around you. Allow your child to choose which option they'll use. Role-play the scenario.

3. How does your superhero body feel after defeating the monsters? Lay on the ground with your child to feel your heartbeats. Talk about what might have happened had they chosen the other option.

4. Bonus time—the monsters came back! Try using other objects to defeat the monsters and compare them.

MATERIALS:

SAFE OBJECTS, SUCH AS FOAM BLOCKS, PILLOWS, AND BLANKETS

GET CREATIVE: Look the part! Dress up like superheroes and create a role-play scenario.

SCAVENGER HUNT ADVENTURE

Children are naturally curious creatures. They want to investigate every-thing. Go on an adventure to discover objects within their environment while challenging their imaginations on how to use the objects.

MATERIALS:

COMMON HOUSEHOLD OBJECTS (TOOTHBRUSH, GLOVE, MUG, ETC.)

STEPS:

1. Invite your child on a scavenger hunt adventure.

2. Name one thing at a time that your child must find around the house as fast as they can. This will get their body moving!

3. Once they find the object, ask your child to choose two different ways the item they found can be used. Will there be any consequences to using it either way?

4. Now have your child find the next item. Repeat until three to five items are found.

5. Talk about body sensations! Ask your child how their body feels after finding the items. Is their heart beating fast? Did they find some items more quickly than others? Do they feel proud finding the objects?

SIMPLE SWAP: On a sunny day, offer an outdoor scavenger hunt instead.

MY BRAIN BOSS

Our brains tell us how to move, how to feel, how to behave, and so much more. In this activity, little ones will learn more about their masterful brains and how to know when their brain needs a break.

STEPS:

1. Discuss with your little one how our brains are the bosses of our bodies. They help tell us how to move, feel, and talk. Today, we're going to help our brain bosses take breaks. Explain to your child that breaks calm our bodies.

2. Suggest two or three short activities for your child to try that can be calming for their body. For example: coloring, hugging a favorite stuffed animal, or stretching.

3. Have your child try each activity for a minute or two, then tell you how their body feels after each one. Does their body feel calmer or more anxious?

4. After your child tries all the activities, have their boss brain choose their favorite one. Talk to your child about saving these activities in their boss brains for times they have big worries.

MATERIALS:

OPTIONAL: COLORING SUPPLIES, STUFFED ANIMAL

AGE ADAPTATION: Offer three-year-olds 2 or 3 choices, and give four- and five-year-olds 4 or 5 options. If they're visual learners, include pictures to help them remember.

HELPING HANDS, STOMPING FEET

When we pair movements—also known as nonverbal cues—with decision-making, we can empower children to know how it feels to make healthy choices.

MATERIALS:

KID-FRIENDLY WRITING UTENSIL

STRIPS OF PAPER

PLASTIC JAR

OPTIONAL: DECORATIONS FOR EXTERIOR OF JAR

STEPS:

1. Together, discuss different ideas and situations that make your child happy or unhappy.

2. Choose at least three happy and three unhappy ideas, and write each one on a strip of paper. Place them in the plastic jar. If desired, your child can decorate the jar with stickers or markers. Have your child shake up the jar—maybe even do a dance!

3. Take turns choosing a strip of paper from the jar. Choose whether to clap to indicate "helping hands" or stomp to indicate "stomping feet," depending on how the idea makes you each feel.

4. Repeat until you have each taken three turns. Keep going if your child is enjoying the game!

GET CREATIVE: Young children love having independence. Your child can create new hand or body gestures for this game, instead of clapping and stomping.

MESSINESS:	PREP TIME:	ACTIVITY TIME:
0	None	5 to 7 minutes

MY FIRST WEATHER REPORT

Feelings aren't permanent, and neither is the weather. This activity helps little ones explore and take ownership of their emotions in a creative way.

STEPS:

1. Discuss with your child how our emotions can change just like the weather does, and how neither of these lasts forever.

2. Together, create your very own weather report to show the weather outside *and* inside your bodies.

3. Start by pairing each weather word with an emotion word. For example, sunny might go with joy and happiness, while windy might stand in for feeling anxious and unsure.

4. To create your weather report, go outside together to check the weather. Your child can choose to write a word or draw a picture to show the weather outside.

5. Next, check in on your bodies' "inner weather." You and your child can choose to write or draw a picture. Does their weather feel the same as outside? You can model this, too, by creating your own weather report.

MATERIALS:

BLANK PAPER

COLORING SUPPLIES

SIMPLE SWAP: Switch up the time of day the next time you do this activity. How does the weather—inside and out—change at different times of the day?

RESOURCES

Websites

Committee for Children: CFChildren.org
This is a global organization that focuses on childhood social and emotional learning. The website offers helpful resources for parents, caregivers, educators, and helping professionals on several social-emotional topics, too!

Headspace: Meditation for Kids: Headspace.com/meditation/kids
This is a great resource for kids to focus on their body sensations and pair them together with their present emotions. There's always a free trial!

PBS Kids for Parents: PBS.org/parents
A great place for social-emotional resources for little ones ranging from ages 2 to 8.

Sesame Street in Communities: SesameStreetInCommunities.org
This is your one-stop shop for many social-emotional topics. One of my favorite things is an app called Breathe, Think, Do, which is also the title of a breathing exercise to build resiliency in children. SesameStreet.org/apps

Books for Kids

The Invisible String by Patrice Karst (Ages 4 to 8)
This is a sweet story that helps kids connect their bodies with tough feelings.

Mindfulness for Little Ones by Heidi France (Ages 2 to 5)
This book is the perfect complement to the activity book you're reading now. Mindfulness and co-regulation go together like peanut butter and jelly.

Roaring Mad Riley by Allison Szczecinski (Ages 5 to 7)
This story brings the emotional regulation skills kids have practiced to life with fun dinosaur friends. Check out how Riley overcomes her big emotions when things don't go her way.

Books for Parents and Caregivers

The Five Love Languages of Children by Gary Chapman, PhD, and Ross Campbell, MD
This book can help you discover your child's primary love language, supporting healthy social-emotional growth and development.

REFERENCES

"Ages & Stages: Making Choices." Scholastic. Accessed November 10, 2021. Scholastic.com/teachers/articles/teaching-content/ages-stages-making -choices.

Greene, Ross W., and J. Stuart Ablon. *Treating Explosive Kids: The Collaborative Problem-Solving Approach.* New York: The Guilford Press, 2006.

Handel, Steven. "The Physical Sensations Behind Emotions: Improving Awareness of the Mind-Body Connection." The Emotion Machine. October 7, 2021. Accessed November 30, 2021. TheEmotionMachine.com/the-physical -sensations-behind-emotions-improving-awareness-of-the-mind-body -connection.

Murray, Desiree W., Katie Rosanbalm, Christina Christopoulos, and Amar Hamoudi. *Self-Regulation and Toxic Stress Report 1: Foundations for Understanding Self-Regulation from an Applied Developmental Perspective.* Washington, DC: Office of Planning, Research and Evaluation, Administration for Children and Families, US Department of Health and Human Services, 2015.

Ward, Christina M. "What Are Normal Attention Spans for Children?" The Kid's Directory Family Resource Guide. July 28, 2020. Accessed December 1, 2021. Kids-Houston.com/2020/08/21/what-are-normal-attention-spans -for-children.

INDEX

Acknowledgments

This book could not have been written without the tireless nights shared with my partner and three fur babies. Thank you also to the remarkable children who inspired these activities. So much gratitude to the team at Healing Pathways of Houston for holding down the fort when I couldn't. And, finally, thanks and love to my family and friends—writing this book kept me very busy, but I promise I'm still around!

About the Author

 Mallory Striesfeld, MS, LPC, is a practicing mental health therapist in Houston, Texas. She received her master's degree in marriage and family therapy from Our Lady of the Lake University in 2014. Mallory works with children and their families, and believes we're all kids at heart. She first discovered her fondness and passion for play therapy while working at nonprofit mental health organizations.

Mallory is the founder of Healing Pathways of Houston, a collaborative team of mental health professionals serving the Houston, Texas, area. She also supervises graduate counseling students, offers presentations, and guest lectures locally.

Though she's not a mom to human children quite yet, she has three amazing fur babies—Hannah, Stark, and Logan. She also has a human partner who helps her self-regulate often. She is a daughter, sister, aunt, friend, and proud member of the type I diabetes (TID) community.

Find Mallory on Facebook and Instagram at @healingpathwayshouston and online at HealingPathwaysHouston.com.

About the Illustrator

Tanya Emelyanova was born in Siberia, where she studied advertising and mass communication. But since drawing has always been her true passion, she embarked on an illustration and pattern design career. Now she is working from her home studio in Valencia. Tanya loves to create cute and funny characters and illustrations for children's books and magazines, printed art, and more, combining both digital and analog materials.